PAPER CUTS

—BEST WISHES
—Dan WASSERMAN
'03

Dan Wasserman

PAPER CUTS

The American Political Scene
from Bush to Newt

FOREWORD BY JIM HIGHTOWER

IVAN R. DEE   CHICAGO

These cartoons first appeared in the *Boston Globe* and are here reprinted with the *Globe*'s permission.

Library of Congress Cataloging-in-Publication Data:
Wasserman, Dan.
    Paper cuts : the American political scene from Bush to Newt / Dan Wasserman ; foreword by Jim Hightower.
       p.   cm.
    ISBN 1-56663-092-4
    1. United States—Politics and government—1989–1993—Caricatures and cartoons. 2. United States—Politics and government—1993—Caricatures and cartoons. 3. Editorial cartoons—Massachusetts—Boston. 4. American wit and humor, Pictorial.
I. Title.
E881.W37   1995
973.928'0207--dc20   95-35107

To Christine, Anika, and Sam

CONTENTS

FOREWORD
by Jim Hightower

If you're looking for the news behind the news from Washington—
who's really doing what to whom, and why—forget the newspaper
pundits, CNN, and the Internet. The source you want is Dan
Wasserman, a direct descendant of those principled, hell-raising,
democratic pamphleteers of America's revolutionary beginnings.
Like our forebears, Wasserman takes the unvarnished truth and nails
it to the wall every day for us to see. He even draws a picture of it.

Wasserman grabs you with his humor—but that's just so he can get
inside your head and question your preconceived notions. Even those
who disagree with him have to stop and think. He's filled with
unconventional wisdom, and in daily doses he's such a delightful anti-
dote to those phony "populists" in politics and the media who try to
use the spreading anger and alienation of Americans to turn them
against one another: "You out of work? It's because of those minori-
ties...or those women...or immigrants...or unions...or environ-
mentalists...or homosexuals...or liberals...THEM!"

I was born at night, but it wasn't last night. If "they" are taking so
much from us, why are we *all* falling farther and farther down? Maybe
our country's corporate bosses and bankers and Wall Street specula-
tors and global spoilers have us worrying about one another so we
won't think to look up at them.

The privileged and the powerful are the target of Wasserman's pen.
Yes, he takes on the major political personalities of our time, but he

goes beyond them to throw the spotlight on real-life villains who "downsize" and export our jobs, who corporatize every aspect of our culture, and who separate our economy into bosses and the rest of us.

Yet, as you'll see in this great collection, Wasserman's message does not depress or breed cynicism (which leads only to defeatism). Instead *Paper Cuts* radiates his deep sense of optimism and expectation that change is possible. He practices what I preach on my national radio talk show: Don't just get agitated, get *agitating.*

Even if you don't live near Wasserman's home paper, the *Boston Globe,* you know his cartoons because they're syndicated and reprinted. And because all across the country, activists regularly clip a "Wasserman" to reproduce in their community newsletter, pamphlet, or whatever, lending his sharp insight and drawing skill to their grassroots movement. That's why I say Dan Wasserman is a pamphleteer with solid roots in democratic ideals.

In *Paper Cuts* he'll take you from the last days of Ronald Reagan to the sprouting of Newt Gingrich, two guys who have moved our nation from Tweedledumb to Tweedledumber in a single decade. You'll enjoy the Wasserman wit that drives the powerful crazy (for some of them, that's a pretty short ride).

So laugh and learn, and let's work together toward America's true revolutionary values: economic fairness, social justice, and equal opportunity for all.

*Jim Hightower is a nationally syndicated radio host
and commentator with a populist perspective.
He broadcasts from Austin, Texas.*

INTRODUCTION

A good editorial cartoon is like good graffiti. Not ugly, boring graffiti where someone sprays his name in neon on a subway car, but spontaneous, head-turning graffiti.

I saw one of my favorite examples in Washington, D.C., in 1980. Daily I drove by a wall where some electoral dropout had sprayed in large black letters, "NOBODY FOR PRESIDENT!" It dominated the intersection for weeks until the morning after Election Day and the news of Ronald Reagan's triumph. Passersby were greeted by a spray-painted addendum written just below in a different script that read, "You Got Him."

The most haunting graffiti I've seen was in the streets of Buenos Aires in the early '80s when the Argentine military was "disappearing" leftists, democrats, and other undesirables. Brave artists took to the streets under the cover of darkness with life-size silhouettes of human figures. They sprayed along the edges of the stencils, leaving groups of ghostly outlines symbolizing the missing. The effect was harrowing.

Editorial cartooning explores the space between the Washington wiseguy and the Argentine artists. Done well, it thrives on the immediacy of its commentary and the staying power of its imagery. It is slightly more respectable than graffiti, and less likely to get one arrested. But people offended by the message of particular cartoons often consider them acts of vandalism.

Graffiti artists, of course, have the luxury of striking when the spirit moves them. Cartoonists for daily newspapers work on a somewhat more regular schedule and appear in a predictable space, wrapped in the institutional presence of their newspaper. But in exchange for spontaneity we gain (one hopes) continuity, discipline, and an ongoing relationship with readers, not to mention a salary.

This collection is taken from the last eight years, from the waning days of the Gipper to Newt's New Wave. It includes the cartoons that I still like and that are still intelligible without recourse to explanatory captions. Like graffiti, editorial cartoons often have a very short shelf life. They are necessarily "of the moment." Some of the best and most biting cartoons, because of their attachment to time and place, lose their meaning within days as political reality changes or the spotlight shifts elsewhere.

I've made one exception—the cartoon of a teddy bear averting its eyes. It was drawn April 19, 1995, the day of the bombing of the Federal Building in Oklahoma City as I watched television images of dead and wounded children being pulled from the wreckage of the blast. The bear is an image I would probably have rejected as too maudlin in any other circumstance, but on that day it seemed an apt expression of the country's collective horror. It clearly struck a chord among readers because it elicited more requests for copies than any drawing I've done.

The public figures who are the subject of many of these cartoons are for the most part accustomed to the rough and tumble of American politics and often display their cartoon likenesses with pride.

There are, of course, exceptions. Just after he was named Bush's chief of staff, John Sununu's family refused to speak with a *Globe* reporter because one of my drawings depicted him as a snarling cur. There is also the opposite problem—politicians whose self-absorption won't allow them to stop looking into the mirror of editorial cartoons. The following is an actual White House letter, authorized and mailed on White House stationery to dozens of daily newspaper cartoonists around the country:

THE WHITE HOUSE

WASHINGTON

March 18, 1994

Dear Cartoonist:

Every week, the White House News Analysis Department compiles and then distributes political cartoons to key White House officials. These "Clintoons" provide comic relief for many White House staffers. Numerous interns and volunteers gather and collect the cartoons from various newspapers nationwide, and this process can become highly time consuming and tedious. To make this process more efficient, we are asking cartoonists to submit copies of political cartoons directly to our office. If you agree to do this, please have your cartoons mailed to:

The White House
Office of News Analysis
Washington, D.C. 20500-0162

Should you have any questions, please contact Cara Levy at (202) 456-7151. She will get in touch with you soon to follow up on this letter. We also encourage you to inform other cartoonists of our interest. Thank you for your assistance, and we look forward to working with you in the future.

Sincerely,

Keith Boykin

Keith Boykin
Special Assistant to the President
& Director of News Analysis

I replied:

The Boston Globe

P.O. BOX 2378 BOSTON, MA 02107-2378 (617) 929-2000

March 22, 1994

Keith Boykin
Special Assistant to the President
& Director of News Analysis
White House
Washington, DC

Dear Keith Boykin:

Thank you for your letter of March 18. I would be happy to comply with your request, provided we can work out a reciprocal arrangement.

Every week cartoonists across the country sort through numerous news outlets to identify the Clinton Administration's latest gaffes, missteps and broken promises in order to assemble the material for what you refer to as 'Clintoons.' As you can no doubt appreciate, this process can become highly time consuming and tedious. To make this process more efficient, cartoonists are asking that you send advanced notice of White House blunders and bungling directly to our offices.

We also encourage you to inform other offices of the Executive Branch of our interest. Thank you for your assistance, and we look forward to working with you in the future.

Sincerely,

Dan Wasserman

Dan Wasserman
Editorial Cartoonist

The White House didn't accept my offer and will therefore have to settle for a copy of this book. Two sections should be of particular interest: "I Feel Your Campaign" centers on the last two and the current race for the White House, and "The Foundering Fathers" depicts the wooly world of Washington, D.C.

Other sections include: "Pre-existing Conditions," on the state of our health and health-care system; "Domestic Disturbances," on our national traumas over race, religion, and sex; "Downwardly Mobile," on corporate downsizing of our work lives and corporate intrusion into our private lives; and "Do Your People Have Oil?" on the calculus of the new world order. "Boston Beans" is a glimpse into the machinations of Massachusetts politics.

I'm indebted to my co-workers at the *Globe,* readers who write, readers who rant, and my editors—Marty Nolan, Loretta McLaughlin, H. D. S. Greenway, and, most of all, the late Kirk Scharfenberg.

1
I Feel
Your Campaign

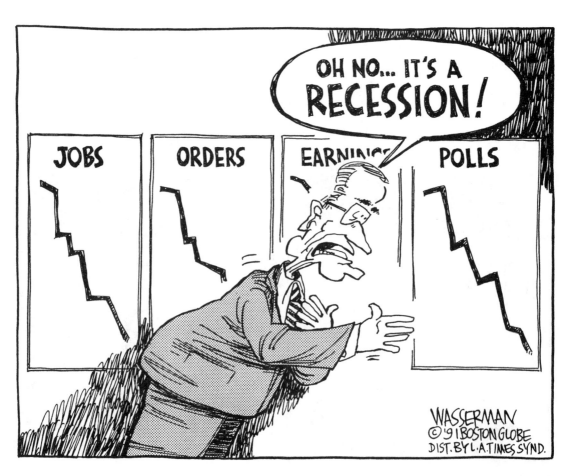

ANGLING FOR THE ANGER VOTE

CUOMO CROSSING THE DELAWARE

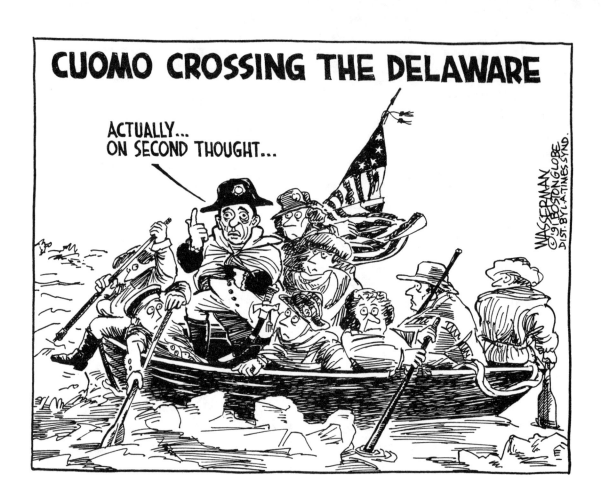

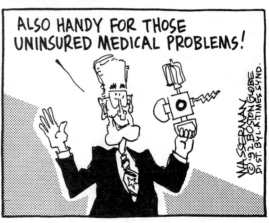

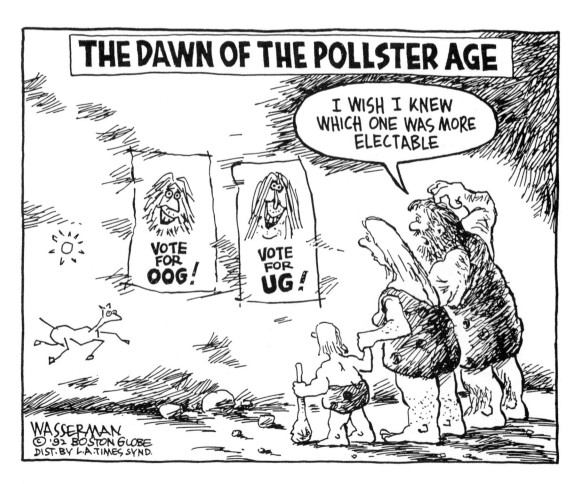

THERE ONCE WAS A FORMER CHIEF SNOOP...

CIA DIR. BUSH

... WHO CLAIMED HE WAS OUT OF THE LOOP

IRAN CONTRA

BUT OTHERS NOW SAY HE WAS BRIEFED ALL THE WAY

MIGHT HE FIND HIMSELF OUT ON THE STOOP?

WASSERMAN © '92 BOSTON GLOBE
DIST. BY L.A.T.S.

AND THAT CONCLUDES OUR '92 CAMPAIGN SPECIAL—
"THE WIMP, THE WONK AND THE WACKO."

WASSERMAN
© '92 BOSTON GLOBE
DIST. BY L.A. TIMES SYNDICATE

33

34

2
The Foundering Fathers

LET'S SEE— FORECLOSURES FOR THE FARMERS...

DRUG TESTS FOR TRANSPORTATION WORKERS...

AN ANTI-ABORTION LAWSUIT FOR THE LADIES...

MORE T.V. JUNK FOR THE KIDDIES...

AND SOCIAL SECURITY CUTOFFS FOR THE OLD FOLKS.

AS WE SAY IN SHOW BIZ— ALWAYS LEAVE 'EM LAUGHING

JOHN IS GOING TO HELP ME MAKE THIS A KINDER, GENTLER NATION

GRRRR...

GEORGE BUSH'S ALL-PURPOSE EXPLANATION →

I WAS OUT OF THE LOOP... OR I WAS OUT OF THE ROOM...

OR OUT OF THE BRIEFING... OR IN THE BRIEFING BUT OUT OF THE ROOM...

OR DOING A BRIEF LOOP AROUND THE ROOM...

OR WAS I GROOVING IN MY ROOM WITH A BREW?.. NO...

I KNOW! — I WAS BRIEFLY GROOMING MYSELF IN THE LOO!!

WASSERMAN ©'88 THE BOSTON GLOBE DIST. BY L.A. TIMES SYND.

ALL CONGRESSMEN IN FAVOR OF EASY ACCESS TO HANDGUNS, PLEASE RAISE YOUR HANDS

WASSERMAN ©'88 THE BOSTON GLOBE DIST. BY L.A. TIMES SYND.

NRA

41

BLOOD-THIRSTY GANG TERRORIZES NATION'S CAPITAL!

"ECHOES OF THE '80s" FEDERAL PRISON

WELCOME! YOU'LL LIKE IT HERE. WE'VE GOT A GOOD SETUP.

LEONA HELMSLEY TAKES CARE OF HOUSEKEEPING, MICHAEL MILKEN RUNS THE RACKETS...

JIM BAKKER TENDS TO OUR SPIRITUAL NEEDS, AND IF ANYONE GETS CAUGHT...

ADMIRAL POINDEXTER TAKES THE FALL!

45

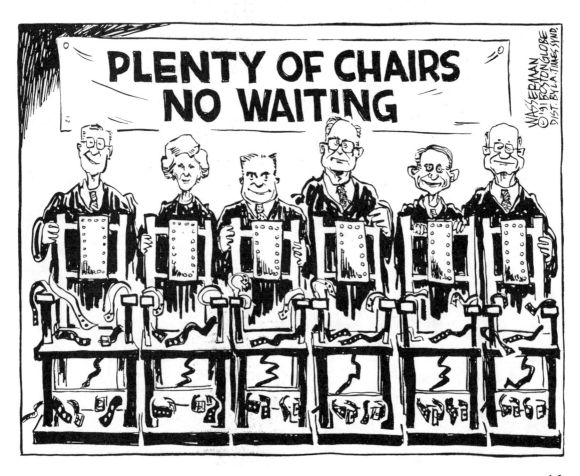

GOSH, GEORGE — IN RECENT YEARS, POVERTY HAS BEEN GOING UP...

FAMILY INCOME HAS BEEN COMING DOWN...

...AND ECONOMIC GROWTH IS WAY OFF.

HOLLYWOOD SURE HAS A LOT TO ANSWER FOR!

I'M NOT SURPRISED THE NAACP OPPOSES MY NOMINATION

THOMAS

THEY'RE A SPECIAL-INTEREST GROUP WITH THEIR OWN AGENDA

THEY'RE OUT OF TOUCH WITH THE REAL CONCERNS OF OUR PEOPLE

WHAT DO THEY KNOW ABOUT THE DAILY LIFE OF THE AVERAGE REPUBLICAN?

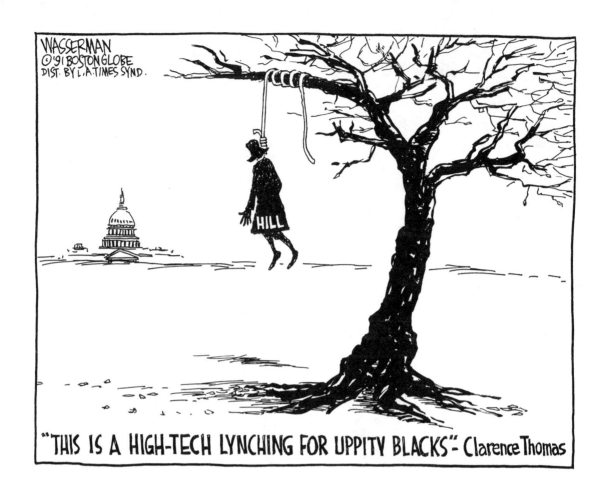

"THIS IS A HIGH-TECH LYNCHING FOR UPPITY BLACKS"- Clarence Thomas

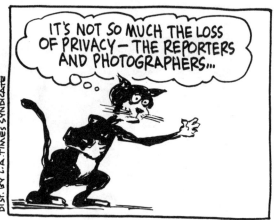

INCREDULOUS RON BROWN

GEN. POWELL'S PHOBIA

53

WELCOME TO "INSIDE THE BELTWAY."
TONIGHT- THE GERGEN APPOINTMENT

FIRST WE'LL TALK WITH THE NEW
DEMOCRATIC ADVISER DAVID GERGEN

THEN WE'LL GET THE REPUBLICAN
VIEWPOINT WITH... DAVID GERGEN

AND FINALLY, AN ANALYSIS FROM
OUR COMMENTATOR... DAVID GERGEN

THE ULTIMATE IMPACT OF NAFTA IS UNKNOWN...

...BUT IT HAS ALREADY AFFECTED TRADING ACTIVITY.

OFFICIALS REPORT AN UPSURGE IN THE BUYING AND SELLING...

...OF MEMBERS OF CONGRESS.

WASSERMAN
© '93 BOSTON GLOBE
DIST. BY L.A.TIMES SYND.

THE PENTAGON PONDERS THE PERILS

OUR FORCES MIGHT GET BOGGED DOWN IN THE BALKANS

OUR ALLIES IN EUROPE MIGHT GET COLD FEET

OUR PUBLIC SUPPORT MIGHT FADE

OUR U.N. COMMANDER MIGHT BE GAY!!

WASSERMAN © '93 BOSTON GLOBE DIST. BY L.A.T.

57

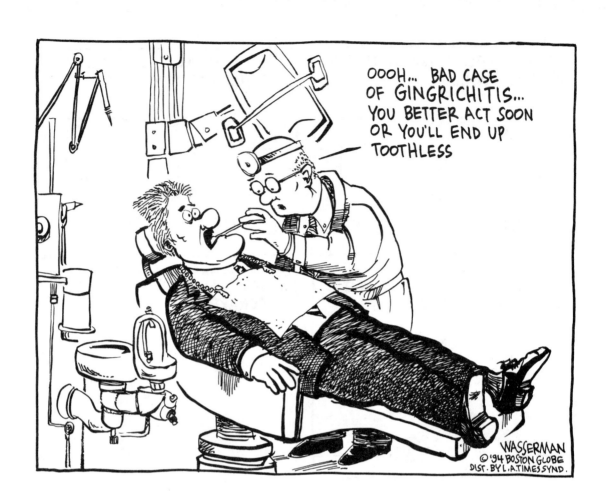

THE SMITHSONIAN AVOIDS CONTROVERSY

3
Downwardly Mobile

HOMELESS TRY NEW WAY TO GET HELP

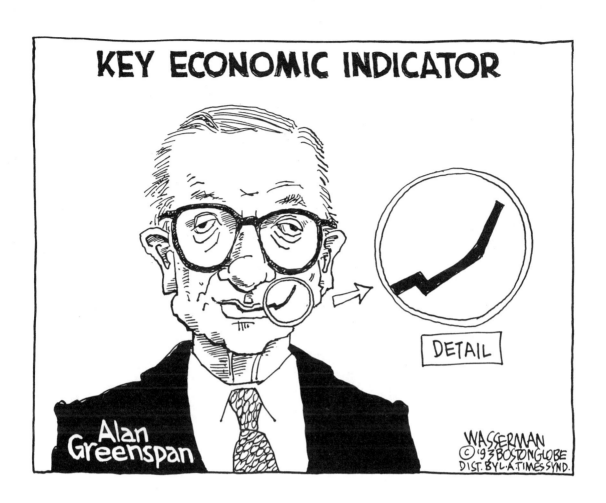

ENTREPRENEURIAL GOVERNMENT

4
Domestic Disturbances

87

HOW WILL AMERICA REACT TO TELEVISED EXECUTIONS?

Ⓐ IT MADE ME RETHINK MY SUPPORT FOR THE DEATH PENALTY.

Ⓑ IT MADE ME RETHINK MY OPPOSITION TO THE DEATH PENALTY.

Ⓒ IT MADE ME RETHINK MY SUPPORT FOR TELEVISION.

Ⓓ HOW COME IT'S NOT INTERACTIVE?

WASSERMAN ©'94 BOSTON GLOBE
DIST. BY L·A·TIMES SYND.

I DON'T UNDERSTAND BLACK PEOPLE — MOST OF THEM THINK O.J. IS INNOCENT...

... AND THEY'RE GIVING MARION BARRY A SECOND CHANCE!

STICKING UP FOR SCOUNDRELS!! HAVE YOU EVER SEEN SUCH A THING?!

NOT SINCE THE NIXON FUNERAL

WASSERMAN ©'94 BOSTON GLOBE
DIST. BY L·A·TIMES SYND.

100

THOSE #©!⚡✦★♄ GOVERNMENT BUREAUCRATS

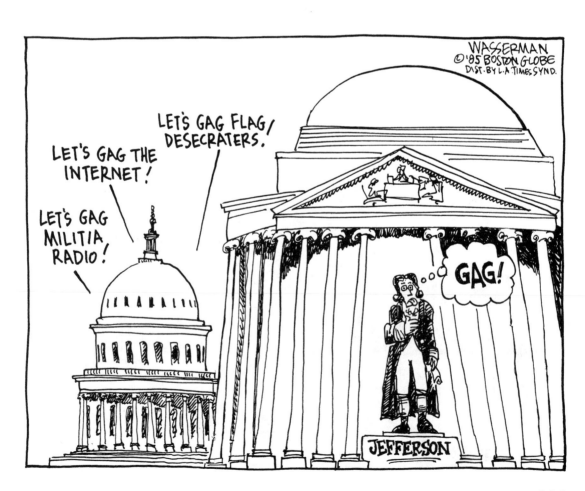

5
Do Your People Have Oil?

FUNDAMENTALISTS SEEK OUT AUTHOR
TO DISCUSS TARNISHING OF THEIR IMAGE

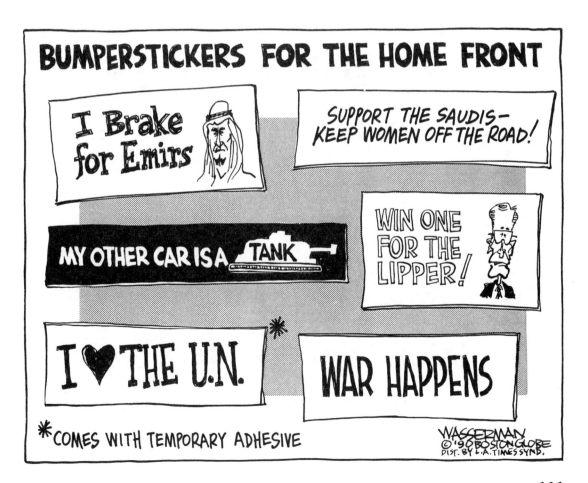

117

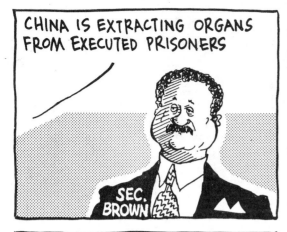

6
Boston
Beans

THE NEW DEMOCRATIC LEADERSHIP

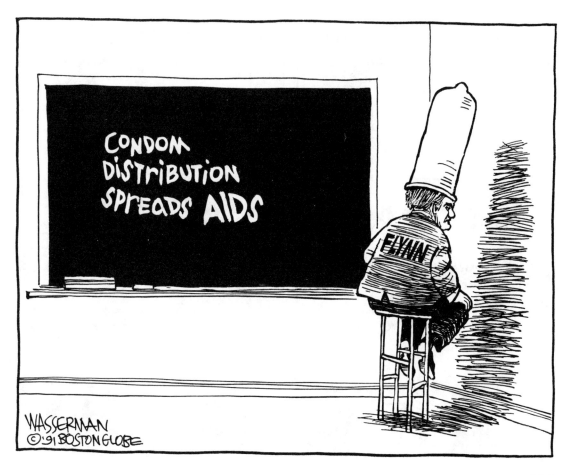

135

GOV. WELD'S NEW SAFETY NET

YES, I'M ANOTHER MASSACHUSETTS DEMOCRAT WITH A GREEK NAME...

TSONGAS

...BUT I'M ALSO PRO-BUSINESS AND PRO-NUCLEAR

SO MY CAMPAIGN IS REALLY A SORT OF GRAND SYNTHESIS...

...UNITING THE LIABILITIES OF BOTH PARTIES

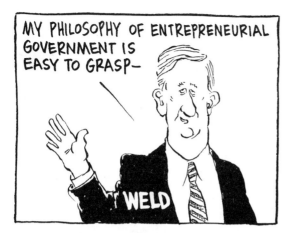

MY PHILOSOPHY OF ENTREPRENEURIAL GOVERNMENT IS EASY TO GRASP—

WELD

PEOPLE ARE MOTIVATED BY THE PROMISE OF MONEY

GOVERNMENT MOTIVATES BUSINESS PEOPLE WITH THE PROMISE OF MORE MONEY...

... AND IT MOTIVATES POOR PEOPLE WITH THE PROMISE OF LESS

WASSERMAN © '91 BOSTON GLOBE

137

139

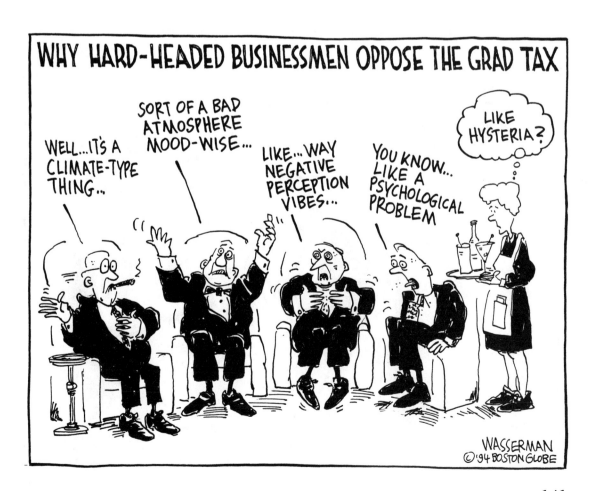

7
Pre-existing Conditions

149

150

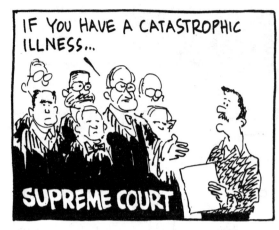